To: Juliet With

C000007010

Dead Lions
Don't Roar

Don't stop roaring!

by:

Tolu' A. Akinyemi

btntowo
31/07/2021 xx

A collection of poetic wisdom for the discerning

First published in Great Britain as a softback original in 2017
This revised and updated edition published in 2020

Typesetting by Word2Kindle

Design by
Jay Thompson (UK Book Publishing)

Published by 'The Roaring Lion Newcastle'
ISBN: 978-1-913636-04-3

Email:
tolu@toluakinyemi.com
author@deadlionsdontroar.com
author@tolutoludo.com

Website:
www.toluakinyemi.com
www.deadlionsdontroar.com
www.tolutoludo.com

ALSO, BY Tolu' A. Akinyemi from 'The Roaring Lion Newcastle'

"Unravel your Hidden Gems" (A collection of Inspirational and Motivational Essays)

"Dead Dogs Don't Bark" (A collection of Poetic Wisdom for the Discerning Series 2)

"Dead Cats Don't Meow" (A collection of Poetic Wisdom for the Discerning Series 3)

"Never Play Games with the Devil" (A collection of Poems)

"Inferno of Silence" (A collection of Short Stories)

"A Booktiful Love" (A collection of Poems)

Dedication

Dead Lions Don't Roar is dedicated to God Almighty for bestowing unto me numerous gifts and talents, and to my dad, Gabriel Akinyemi, for teaching and mentoring me into the Man I am today.

Contents

Poems

THE DEADS

THE LION

THE DON'TS

THE ROARS

Preface

Dead Lions Don't Roar is a symbolic poetry collection that challenges us to find our unique roar as individuals and take the walk of glory while we are here. The collection has four underlying themes which are hinged on the title: The Deads, The Lion, The Don'ts, and The Roars.

The poems surrounding The Deads have underlying themes of things, relationships, and vices that are dead and harmful, while poems on the theme of The Lion exhibit strong characters and qualities that are worthy of emulation. The Lion is also a devourer—hence the personification of some of these poems might show the other characteristics of the lion.

The underlying themes of the poems The Don'ts bring to light negative attitudes and how we can do things better, while the final section, The Roars, hold poems that show the fierce quality of a lion "Roaring." *Dead Lions Don't Roar* is an eclectic read that takes the reader through varying waves of emotions. The poems in this collection will challenge you to find your own distinct roar. This is a unique form of poetry, as the words are deep-rooted and the book has been written to inspire a change in as many lives as possible. The truth is: we all have talents and gifts. Whether we put them to use or not is the main topic under discussion.

Even in our busy lives and with the tight schedules and commitments in our everyday experiences, any dream we have should not be aborted at the incubation stage. *Dead Lions Don't Roar* will help us to reinvent ourselves in our work, business, relationships, and marriages, and will help us put our talents to good use. *Dead Lions Don't Roar* celebrates life and advocates living a life of purpose. Metaphorically, whether you are a cat, dog, chicken, or rat, as long as you are a living being, you are better off than a dead lion. The lion is the king of the jungle; however, a dead lion is a mere object. Literally speaking, no matter the situation we might be going through in life, as long as there is breath in us, that is an indication that we have great hope for the future. Yes, we do have hope for life, to aspire and dream of a better future. Always remember that the only time you have to leave your footprints on the sands of time is when you are alive. As the title infers, dead lions don't roar.

As you go on to read through the pages of this book which I have written specifically for you, I do hope that you will find it a rewarding experience.

Acknowledgements

To my darling wife and partner, Olabisi, thank you for your inspiration and support, my number one fan. Thanks for taking the time to listen, over and over again, to the poems, and for giving me great feedback and advice during the course of my writing. I will always love you.

A big thank you to my beautiful children, Isaac and Abigail. You lighten up my world and inspire me to live my dreams. I would also like you to know that the world is your oyster. Do not be afraid to live your dreams. Dad will always be there to support you throughout life's journey.

Special thanks to my dad and mum. What a great privilege to learn at your feet. Thanks for teaching me great wisdom. I appreciate your sacrifices, investments, and selflessness, and for being there at every step of the journey.

Special appreciation goes to my siblings, Shola, Seyi and Ireti. Always know that I love you come what may.

Special thanks to my editor, Gabrielina Gabriel, and the team at The Roaring Writer NG. Appreciation also goes to the book designer, Jason Thompson. I am indeed proud of your work.

My huge appreciation to Diane Donovan for a final proofread of this collection.

A special "shout-out" to the poetry editor, Kolabomi Adeko. It's been a joy working with you on this revised edition.

To Nzubechukwu Alutu, my friend for all seasons: I appreciate your friendship and the man that you are.

A final thank you to my creative brand manager Antonia Brindle. Thanks for the amazing work and your relentless effort.

Poems

THE DEADS

Extra Luggage

I left this extra luggage at the terminals,
Terminated our ill-fated relationship
That was moribund
Like a *terminal-ly* ill patient.

I have become deadwood
From the weight of lifting empty men.
This has become a hefty mess
And I draw blanks from staring into emptiness.

I said goodbye at the departure area
To the companion of
Weightless men
And extra luggage.

Moments

Anxiety wells up in my belly,
A stench up my guts
Like the unflushed toilet in the neighbourhood.
Depression pays a visit
And wanders off through the back door
                                    Into thin air.

There are nights when I feel my skin crawl
From doses of fear.
Two, Three, Four—I **can't tell**.
I flounder into wet gardens
With beautiful landscapes
Leaving the gloom (*my gloom*) for dead.

Those dark spaces are real.
Like a drunken man
On a pub crawl,
I killed my demons.
One, Two, Three, **Knockout.**
I wander off into dreamland.

Fire In The Tower

Tower of Chaos,
Chaos the World can't overcome.
Burning blazes,
A Blaze the World can't comprehend.

Children weeping
Grief the World can't overcome.
None was spared
A fire the World can't comprehend.

Mobiles ringing,
Ringing aloud from the rooftops
Drowning voices,
Voices laden with sorrow,
Sorrow too hard to bear.

No escape, no route to
Escape an arduous task,
A task too difficult to bear.
A raging Fire,
Fire the smoke jumpers can't comprehend.

(Dedicated to the memory of the victims of the unfortunate fire incident
in Grenfell Tower, London, on Wednesday, 14 June, 2017.)

Half-men, Half-gods

We are half-men,
Half-gods,
Spirit beings wandering till we reach
A dead end.

Death is the end
Of the sojourn. Our sojourn.
There were days of black pots,
Black dirty pots
That cooked meals that looked like
Burnt offerings.

We died. We lived. And we died again.

That was purpose.

If Men Were God

If Men were God
There would be no more us.
Long dead and buried,
Forgotten with the times
As an atonement for our sins.

If Men were God
Our epitaph would have been laid
With their sanctimonious eeriness.
Coming out from the inner chambers of their court
With gleeful laughter in their cheeks
They shout crucify him.

If Men were God,
How dare you aspire for success
Without their seal of approval?
A journey they undertook for three decades
You dared to achieve in five years.

If Men were God,
Judgment would be immediate,
Mercy a no-no,
No second chances,
No reprieve for failure and mistakes.

The Marketplace

The World is a marketplace,
Different wares on display,
A continuous journey
Like wanderers trudging on the Sahara.

Death, the halt to the many troubles.
A home, no one can call
All work and toil
Till Death puts a stop to it.

Aunty Banke

Her words were fire and thunder
Hail and brimstone
Her temper was dwarf-like,
Short. Short like a fuse.

Aunty Banke was carnage
Like a survivor of car wreckage.
She killed him without a sword.
He lost the war and was drowned

In the ocean of negative words.

(**Banke:** A name given to a female child in Nigeria.)

The Tongue

The great warrior
Was brought to naught
In the little dingy room.

He was a giant with phenomenal strides.
His fall was similar to the case
Of David defeating Goliath.

His nemesis was the tongue,
That little brutish fierce weapon,
His news spread like wildfire set off by the blazing sun.

His misfortune found home in strange mouths.
He was a victim of jungle justice;
Not the type meted out to petty thieves.

Wagging tongues like a dog's tail,
He was killed by the small mighty armoury
Cocooned in the mouth.

Villain

I was treasured like precious eggs
Before the break-up
And he made me a villain.

He grew flowers
And thorns in his garden of love.
The thorns soon outgrew the flowers.

That day
Our love disappeared
And evaporated like boiling water.

Who Will Wake Me Up?

Who will wake me up?
This seems a nightmare.
I was your one and only
The oxygen of your life

The love of your youth
A dream, it seems to me—
A dream soon to be forgotten.
The days are long.

And the nights are dark.
Who will wake me up?
And tell me it was all a dream.

Lack Of Money

The absence of Money is the root of all evil.
Money in itself is not evil.
The Quest to fill the Void
Brings the evil out of men.

The lack of money was the cornerstone
That sent the neighbourhood into mourning
Poverty is a monster-
A deadly monster, like a fired-up actor in a blockbuster movie.

Money flies on wings like an eagle
Soaring into high heavens
On a journey of *"no return"*.
We feel the weight of silence on our tender necks
Like a graveyard- a somber graveyard.

(Dedicated to the memory of my maternal grandmother, whose words
of wisdom on money I will never forget. She said, and I quote, "Money
says that in my absence, no one is permitted to make any form of planning.")

I Wrote

I wrote to her
Why I dote on her.
She's been smitten in love;
It's written over her.

She's bold to say it's all a lie.
As cold as Ice she tends to be.
She holds the aces,
I wear the braces.

I wrote to her
Why I am smitten in love.
She's been bitten before,
It's written all over her.

Lost In Time

I forgot you in time,
Those times
That were once tender moments.

I lost you in a season
Those seasons
Where we truly blossomed...

I lost you forever
Looking forward to
Forever without you.

Cupcake

She was **history**
Quickly forgotten as part of **his story**.
Seemed like a fairytale
Until she wagged a fiery tail
To the card swipes for Gucci
And Dolce & Gabbana
And her shopping list from Vanity Square.

She was hit and miss:
Insta Slay Queen doesn't give bliss.
Her taste was finicky,
Left my mate panicky.

She lived rent-free in his heart
And his wallet before she was ousted.

Brainwashed

I have been brainwashed from the pulpit.
I built a castle in the sands of denial.
Men dined with God
Or gods, or whatever they triggered
From their well-rehearsed storylines
That kept the fountain flowing and
The oil of grace in abundance.

One word became a ton of words
That built walls so high.
I became a fragment
Withering away like a shadow.

The Past

In the garden of the past were weeds and thorns.
Seeds were planted in the present-day.
Weeds and seeds fight for survival
For the future.

Weeds sprout like touts
Fighting off seeds that count
As the harvest–
The harvest of despair and regrets.

If Men Were God - 2

If Men were God
The Titanic would be unsinkable.
We would never die, but would all go to heaven.
The World would forever be in chaos,
Blood shedding in bucket loads to atone for our sins.

If Men were God
We would forever wave the planes in the sky;
At best, say goodbye to friends at the terminals.
No redemption, No salvation.

If Men were God,
The big edifices we call 'offices' would be pipe dreams.
Instead of shirts there would be sack cloths.
There would be no rags to riches story:
All we would murmur is 'my destiny'.

If Men were God,
No voice, no talent
No hope for a better tomorrow,
Blown away like a candle in the wind.

Dead Lions

Dead lions are lifeless
Until they receive an awakening
That kicks them out of somnolent.

There are days when greatness gives mediocrity
A kicking.
A fierce tango occurs.

Awake, ye fierce Lion,
Before your dreams kiss the dust
Of death.

Interlope with those great kings past
Who bestrode the jungle
Like a colossus.

Dead Lions Don't ***Roar***.
Idle People don't ***soar***.

THE LION

Dead Lions Don't Roar

Dead lions don't roar.
As tranquil as the still waters,
Their legendary status is now history—
A history soon to be forgotten.

In the graveyard lay many unsung heroes.
Six feet under the ground, therein abide great potentials
Depriving the World of the benefit of their ideas.
We suffer not for lack of talent.

Many a talent bestrode the earth
Like buzzing bees besieging the honeycomb.
The best of men have been laid to rest
To rest with ideas confined within.

The talented musician
with no song to his name
Was buried with his gift
And talent in harmony.

Use your gifts while you can,
As dead lions don't roar.
The memories of them do fade away;
Do fade away with the eras.

Heroes

To our heroes past,
Let's hoist this flag at half mast.
We salute the sweat bands.
Prodigious, we had you in our ranks.

You were our heroes.
Your names are like an anthill
Dancing lullabies through this landscape.
Your spectacular feats

Leave your smattering footprints
Evergreen in our hearts.
One epitaph amongst many reads
'Chief Obafemi Awolowo, the crusader of free education.

To the heroes and **heroines** of the past,
The harbinger of future hope.'

Mother Or Monster-In-Law

How I longed for the love of a mother,
Even the one who bathed me with blood
And carried me for nine months.
At the sound of my wedding bells
I thought I had gotten double for my trouble.
Nay! I was in for a shocker
As the mother has turned into the monster.
She sows discord between me and my rib,
Never wants me to enjoy the joy that she never experienced.
She calls me barren even when I am fertile,
Always finds faults and can never be pleased.
I have been turned into a slave in my home.
I fret at the sight of this monster.
She chants to the rooftops about how my scavenging
And gold-digging mission will fail.
She was never told I was born with the God-spoon;
The spoon that never runs dry.
How I despise this monster
That never sees anything good in everything;
Whose fault-finding mission the MI6 will envy.
Who will help me take this monster away?
So I can live in bliss with my heart-throb.

(I dedicate this poem to all those who endured their marriages and lost their marriages to the prying eyes of a mother-in-law turned monster-in-law. To all those folks out there who attribute the failure of their marriage to a supposed mother-in-law, I dedicate this poem to you.)

27

Bolaji

Maybe there is more to a name.
Every name has a meaning.
Sister Bolaji, the lead chorister in my former church,
Looks as beautiful as her name sounds.

Cynthia and Florence, my African sisters,
Asked Sister Bolaji, in utter glee
"Why do people call you BJ?"
As it reminds them of the trumpet blowing.

Sister Bolaji laughed derisively.
How stupid not to think,
Indeed, that there is more to a name.
Truly, the World has lost its innocence.

(Bolaji is a unisex Yoruba (a tribe in Nigeria) name meaning "wake up with wealth.")

"The M-22's"

The news headline makes a gory viewing
From Brussels to Paris to London.
Bombs they throw at us,
Raping the World of its innocence,
Destruction in its wake an aftertaste
To make us tremble.
Shudder, we don't,
Cowering not being a route on our map.
As Love trumps hate,
United we stand in our beliefs,
United we stand in our grief,
United we stand against the forces of evil,
United We Stand.

(Written in the aftermath of the Westminster Bridge attack (March 22 2017) and Manchester bombing attack (May 22 2017), this poem is dedicated to all the men, women and children who lost their lives during these unfortunate incidents.)

Extraordinary Names

We both drink from the fountain of poetry
And sniff through the deified pages of
Paperbacks.

There are days I don the garment
Of a traffic warden redirecting
Passengers to the alternative route.

At other times, I act as a compass of love.
My head whispers to my heart,
Count me out of rivalries.

Google goes into a frenzy: how do we
Differentiate these extraordinary names?
These poets.

There is a thin line between love and hate,
Kindred and hatred.
A shared name can be an albatross.

Virtuous Woman

Women come in all shapes and sizes
With grace and carriage to envy.
Humility, a virtue.
Her honour, none can take.
Her crown, all can see;
A pride to the one who calls her queen.
Treasure her when you have one to call your own.

2face

Not the popular Nigerian musician,
The Sister who lies between the Angelic and the Devil,
The wife material in the daytime and the devil reincarnate at
Night-time.
Her love for the fast lane seems to be the culprit.
Bring home a wife, my mother said.
She would have been the perfect choice,
If only there was no other face to her.

My Mother

My Mother.
Her husband calls her blessed,
Her children's delight.
Looking for that virtuous woman?
Wander not afar
She lived in our time.

My Mother,
A pillar of support to all and sundry
The steady root behind the Iroko tree.
She arises in the morning with strength and valour.
Peace and tranquillity she brings to bear.

My Mother:
Dad's answered prayers
A blessing to her clan
Lover of God and his creations.

My Mother,
Retired but not tired.
How she loves wisdom and the quest for knowledge.
A teacher of teachers.
My mother, my pride.

(**Iroko tree:** Iroko is a large hardwood tree from the west coast of tropical Africa that can live up to five hundred years.)

This poem is a tribute to my darling mother. I celebrate your wonderful and unblemished career in the civil service, and on behalf of all the children you taught and the lives you shaped and molded, I celebrate you always.

Gemma

Gems are rare.
Value and substance, they depict
A montague no one can crush,
A princess to treasure.

Only the kings can have
Not a sham or a fallacy.
Gems are precious,
Meekness and kindness an attribute.

Let it be known
A Gem lived in our time.

Dedicated to Gemma Montague. Don't stop believing in yourself.

The Married Bachelor

The married bachelor with roving eyes
And tasty eyeballs
was like a thirsty camel at the waterfront.

He was married only by the dotted lines
Of his marriage certificate
And his askew signature.

He was a tenant in the hearts of spinsters
Leaving a legacy of early trimester
And his marriage in a haze of siesta.

The husband material is no longer an option,
The single sisters open their mouth agape.
"We hoped he was still single and searching," they chorused
Aloud.

No ring on the finger, no way to know.
A rope on his finger will do some good
To keep the prying eyes off the man.

The Special One

A folklore hero among modern-day managers,
The darling of blues of London—
If the fans are quick to forget your legacy,
Remember they sang your name aloud.

To the high heavens, they sang your name
In summer and winter,
Through rain and shine.
History will be kind to the special one
That helped the Club in leaps and bounds.

Dedicated to Jose Mourinho. Your name will never be forgotten for generations to come.

Growing Old

Hard to unwind the clock,
Clock of life moving so fast.
Once I was young,
Strong and agile,
Many memories to cherish.
Accomplished quests as a bonus.
Slowly but surely life is fizzling,
My bones frail and nimble,
Counting down the days,
If I had a choice,
I will always choose to stay
Stay forever young.

The Thieving Politician

Our commonwealth flew on wings
To safe havens as the proceeds of crime.
Our state budgets walked on water
Into oblivion,
Criss-crossing oceans
Into political lords' accounts.

I grew up seeing politicians from the
Binoculars of greed and the spectacles of oppression.
Did you see "Alams", the thieving politician
Who disguised himself as a gele-tying woman
And got a presidential pardon
And Uncle James, the one who found home
Behind bars in foreign lands
And was made a deity upon arrival.

Our godfathers were punished by foreign cohorts
And political enemies. That was gospel!
We brought them home with singing praise dirges:
Fireworks, white horses,
Talking drums,
And Chieftaincy titles.

Our politicians have become fine specimens
Of the art of treasury pilferage
And lootocracy in public office
In financial institutions across the world.

Leo Woman

A Royal titivation
Golden Hair
Gait of a Queen
Airs and attitude.

Bold as a lioness
A repository of Confidence
Eloquence not afar
Beauty with Brains.

Her Husband's delight
A defender of her Children
An armory of love and sacrifice
Audacious and tenacious.

Raise a glass for the Leo Woman.

Dedicated to my Darling Wife Olabisi, Sola Adewunmi, and all Leo
Women the world over.

Crime Busters

We are crime busters.
Our gardens are scattered with thorns
Of humongous words.

We build homes in skyscrapers
On-boarding. Off-boarding. On the trail of
Negative news like cow dung stench.

In London, New York, Berlin and those forgotten cities
We uncover global laundromats
Tactically like those dirty laundry mats.

We go to war behind big screens
Against money launderers and
Corporate robbers. *Executhieves* and *legislooters.*

Talk dark money and Russian money
Like oil dripping,
Haunting us like sour honey.

I'm living the dream
Similar to the moonlight tales
You watched on prime-time TV.

I'm a fraud buster,
The nemesis of dark money flaunting
Crime agents and money mules

Hiding behind the piles of clean money.

Father

A shoulder for all
Bolder than all
Like a soldier on the battlefront
Confronting all of life's many troubles.

Dreams foregone,
Foregone for the greater good.
Sacrifices unending,
Unending for the greater good.

A repertoire of Wisdom,
Wisdom the schools can't teach.
A teacher and a counselor,
Counsel the World can't give.

My father, my defender, a
Defender Real Madrid can't afford.
My father, my friend:
A friend, like no other.

Treasure your father
As his admonishment will carry you farther.

Dedicated to my teacher and counselor, Gabriel Akinyemi, and all the
great fathers worldwide.

Isaac

Image of God, clear.
Son of his mother, true:
A reflection of his father,
A joy of his grandfathers,
Charismatic and full of strength.

My unending laughter,
You are my best gift from God.

Special in a very special way,
Onwards to greater heights you go—
Never back down till you win.

Dedicated to my first son, the beginning of my strength.

The Young Shall Grow

We breeze through life.
Our days are measured by sunrises
And sunsets.

We swam in the pool of innocence.
Honesty was a virtue:
We were bereft of worries.

Fast forward.
We sleep. We eat. We dream.
Night after Night.

We make haste into the future,
Losing the innocence of childhood on the way
Adulthood is a ton of baggage and perturbation.

The Power-Drunk Husband

The power drunk husband is here,
Not a murmur or a sound or
Even a muscle, who can flex?
Not a question, who can ask?

His authority, who can dare?
The slave-girl is just a call away.
A wife she ought to be,
Only in her own mind's eye,
As long as the power-drunk husband is here.

THE DON'TS

Nigerian Prince

The Nigerian prince with vast estates
Even Gates will envy, died long ago.
Yes, he died!

Stop defecating your soggy feces
Of greed and
Building empires from the dust of nothingness.

It takes two to tango.
Crime and greed are entangled
In reaping wealth from the mountain of emptiness.

Stop looking for love in strange places,
Preyed upon by familiar strangers
Like the Nigerian prince.

The familiar Nigerian prince
Who died long ago.

Social Media

Our love language reeks of silence.
We laugh into small screens
And lust after **unknown persons**.

We spend the core of our days
Lost in the sea of gadgets
And build empires out of idleness.

We crave validation, acceptance,
And love from unknown men
Who entered the gateway
Of our heart through the back door.

Our bones are broken,
Hearts shattered from the evil
From the wicked and negative vibes
Of social media.

Who Will Tell Sister Vicky?

With a New Day comes a renewed vigour,
A little flesh and some cleavage as take away,
Still competing with the Spinsters.
Who will tell Sister Vicky to cover up?

We were told by the elders of yore to
Dress the way you want to be addressed.
Beauty, they say, is in the eyes of the beholder.
Who will tell Sister Vicky to cover up?

Is this not Sister Vicky, the wife of my Nigerian brother?
The goods belong to the man who paid her bride price.
Who dares confront Sister Vicky with the honest truth?
Maybe, the man we all call her husband.

Renowned Liar

I love the popular line,
A party without Jollof rice is only a gathering.
The food is so popular, a meltdown occurred.
The liar had just blasphemed the pride of our nation.
A stampede occurred,
Not as the ones of the days of yore.
Stomachs rumbled,
Egos were shaken,
Men and women alike.
A lie taken too far.
Many were traumatized—
Disturbing, to say the least,
The pride of the nation has just been taken to the cleaners.
A chant in the realm of social media:
Crucify him not,
He is the national renowned liar.

Twelve Yards

Everyone buys Aso-Ebi.
They come in different yards and sizes,
Yards and sizes to make beautiful attires.
Beauty without, everyone can see.
I looked out for the beautiful twelve yards of
Beauty within her husband's delight,
The wife material, the desire of men.
Beauty to behold fades with the times.
After the make-up and face-beat come off,
What remains is the inner beauty;
The inner beauty that lasts a lifetime.

(Aso-Ebi is a uniform that is traditionally worn in Nigeria and some West African cultures as an indicator of cooperation and solidarity during ceremonies and festive periods.)

Brother Smart

Who will marry Brother Smart?
The most eligible bachelor in our church,
Single to stupor, if I can say,
Who will save Brother Smart from using
His pension fund to send his children to school?
An emissary from the pastor to the sister he loves.

Big Grammar

Is this poetry?
As clear as broad daylight
With no interwoven words, like a nest of spiderweb.

Complexity and ambiguity
Became bedfellows strung together
By grammar-hopping writers.

I'm that reader skipping between
Gadget screens and these folded pages,
Intermittently, like power outage in my clime.

I'm a victim of the grammar-hopping writer,
The writer who built a home far above us all
In the land of big grammar and interwoven words.

Beauty Is Not Enough

If only beauty was enough,
The spinster next door would have been married off
With curves and vital statistics to envy,
With a face as of an angel.
Heads roll at her passing,
The young and old alike:
Alas, beauty seems no longer enough,
The kind of beauty anonymous to the spinster.

Bucket List

This was on my bucket list:
Get married before the age of thirty.
A wedding band on my finger,
My gait changes like a model on the runway.

The single girls will know
I'm a Mrs— I mean, someone's wife.
I'm banging the door shut in their faces.
Mama's song grew me weary.

I became a shadow
From the reminder of Mister Lagbaja's daughter's wedding.
Every wedding was a solemn reminder
Of the misery of my waning years.

I was haunted by these words:
When will you bring home a man?
Just any man.
One goal ticked off my bucket list.

Where Are The Men?

The boys are on the loose again
Donating milky waters as they deem fit.
Not ready for commitment,
Baby Mamas abound in every nook and cranny
For the reason that the boys are on the prowl again.

Jollof

The Jollof was deuces.
I only had some dosage.
My tummy flowed like it had some juices,
My tongue rolled and I had some bruises.

My head spins like a car with no diesel
I am so happy to do the dishes.

(**Jollof rice,** also called Benachin (Wolof: "one pot"), is a one-pot rice dish popular in many West African countries. This is a unique spicy African rice dish; so spicy, it deserved a poem.)

Dignity Park

Your body is a habitat for strange men
And your skin has marks from all the men
That have found refuge between your thighs
Etched on them.

You know that the different colours of heartbreak
And pain took solace in your heart.
Your formula for love was an afterthought
Trust and thrusting left you on the brink.

Lusting and lost are the watersheds
That left you dangling in space.
You take a walk to dignity park. The gate sign
Reads, "The husband will come
Not by opening your legs to boys and men."

Paradise

Paradise became wastelands
When dreams were punctured like tyres on the bumpy road.
We drank from the spring of fear
And our ships on high seas were named
Rejection
And dejection.

A greener pasture
Was supposed to be our rapture.
We had land allocations in the land of refutation.
Some built houses and others watered barren lands
With offspring of depression
And other connotations of unfortunate ness.

Paradise was what it was—
Paradise, but imagined.

Who Are You?

The gate crasher with no identity,
An A-Grade attaché with no substance within,
Was Paul, we know.
Why gate-crash the party without an invite?

A beating and injury, an addition for their bareness.
No identity, no problem.
A mellow heart all can see—
Bravado! Only for the gallant;

The gallant within and without
Abide in thy tent
Till we know who you are.

Superwoman

There are cities where super women are raised
And men's rights are extinguished
And wane with every passing day.

Let's take lessons of history
From this hallowed chamber
And reflect that mens' rights should not

Be quartered on the altar of feminism.
Let's birth kings
And queens from this throne.

Let's avoid pitfalls of the past
And leave epochal words on these streets
That raising weak boys should not be

A consequence of feminism
To avoid a future struggle of "meninism."

Domestic Violence

Once beaten, always beaten.
Life is for the living,
Run while you can.

No hope in the land of the dead:
Better to be single and alive
Than to be married and living in bondage.

The callous boxer-cum-spouse is in the neighbourhood,
No medals or honours to show for it—
Only dishonour in the eyes of their loved ones.

The Other Room

The puzzle of the other room remains a mystery
Similar to the moonlight tales of old,
A facade none can tell,
An imagination of the tale bearer.
What happens in the other room should not be said outside of the
Other room.

The girl child is befuddled
By the ill-thought commentary of the incoherent one.
The woman who toils to eke a living
Is gobsmacked by the tales of the other room.
They mutter, *"Ignore him.*

He is the mansion owner
In the land of ignorance.
His orchestra of words killed dreams,
Raped the future,
And sentenced the women folk to the other room."

(Inspired by the 15th President of the Federal Republic of Nigeria,
Muhammadu Buhari, after a misunderstanding with his wife, Aisha
Buhari.)

What A Cook

Have you seen tongues wag in adulation
At the dinner table
After devouring a tasty meal?

Our taste buds formed
Like an orchestra of songs.
Hats off to Beecee.

She was top chef.
Her diet was scrumptious.
Our belly danced in the fiesta.

Here is the remix:

My neighbour gave a medal of honour
To his partner for top-notch culinary skills.
She won praises like a gold winner
On the Olympic podium.

She was the greatest, in the sandcastles
Of his imagination,
Until it all fell apart
When the veil of ignorance was lifted
And he awoke from his reverie.

Fashion Police

Why do your colours riot
Like activists on a protest against bad governance?
Say me well to the bloke who knows it all:
Either my way, or no way.
Fashion, they say, is what you make of it:
An unending experiment who can fathom,
A discovery that beguiles even the wise.
Who will tell the fashion police to judge no more?
Until I finish my journey of self-discovery.

Heritage

I'm from the land where we worshipped different gods
Before missionaries showed us the one true God.
I'm from the land where Saturdays are for Owambes
And we keep hope alive even in our misery.

I'm from the land of dreams where visionary men
Took the walk of glory.
Our youths lust after greener pastures
And our best brains take flight in mega-droves.

I'm from the land of broken dreams
Broken things
Broken people
And a foul body language.

I'm from the land where elders are respected and feted
Like iconic symbols on national currency.
I'm from the land of abundance and want
Wealth and poverty, suffering and smiling.

This is my heritage, my history
And story.

People On The Bus

Mark, my Oyinbo friend, once said
People on the bus smell.
Mark has forgotten his past:
That he was once riding on the bus.

Mark is not in the wrong, as it was
In the early morning ride from the Coast road to the business
Park.
People on the bus smell of expensive perfumes,
A smelly miscellany of the world's most expensive fragrances.

The evening ride is a tad different.
Mark might truly be right.
Who am I to question Mark?
The truth is: people everywhere smell.

Mark my words.
Who will help me tell Mark?

(**Oyibo or Oyinbo:** a word used in Nigerian Pidgin, Igbo, and Yoruba to refer to westernized people. In Nigeria it is generally used to refer to a person of European descent or people perceived to not be culturally African.)

All Men Cheat

The swan song makes the sisters happy:
Take it as your fate, they say.
Cheating is in the blood of every man,
A part of their DNA no one can erase.
Who made you the senior advocate for all men?
Only speak for the man in your life
Whose zipper needs to be fastened all day long?

Men are scum.
Men are trashy.
Don't cocoon men in the
Deadwood burlesque you call rapport.
Don't beat men with the stick of your inanity
That made you fall for a one-night stand.

I hear the man who broke her heart whisper.
Not all women hop from bed to bed
Looking for love in bizarre spaces
In the arms of unknown men.

Offering Time

Who will tell the lead organist to stop falling into trances
Or stop seeing revelations
When it's time to give offering and tithes?
It's enough that the pastor has had to bear
the scheme to rob God of his dues.

African Writers

We are African writers,
But we are everything un-African.
Only a minuscule
Write about the trauma of Mother Africa.

I sigh.
Is this not hypocrisy
Or hypocritical,
To beat writers with the stick of westernization?

I sneeze.
I look into the rearview mirror
And I see our novelty
Hidden under the shadows.

I sigh again.
Think music or
Politics
Before we open the chapter of the African writer.

Attitude Is Beauty

The slay queen
Was a fake king,
Plastic like a mannequin.

Iwalewa.
A priceless attitude is golden.
All hail the queen, all hail the mother queen.

She was awoke and a rose.
She was the morning orchid.
She was life and living.

She was the metaphor
And the beginning and the end.
She was *bea-uti-ful*.

Beauty without attitude is a façade,
A disaster waiting to happen,
For the real beauty is a pleasant attitude.

(**Iwalewa:** attitude is beauty)

London

London is hard, they say.
As hard as they make it seem to be,
It's only hard for those who believe.
Let it be to you, according to your thoughts.

London was the land of dreams
Where trains got us to hinterlands
And men of **small** *means* heckled at
Survival till their lives became a parody.

London became the superhero in my all-cast movie.
The train operator says, *"This is the Jubilee Line
To Canary Wharf."*
London became my jubilee land; *"my land of jubilation."*

No Issues

No issues.
No issues.
No issues identified
No matter the issues.

Just say "No issues,
No issues identified."
Issues are in the toilet.
As long as you have the tissues
Then there can't be issues.

No issues.
No issues identified.

(First composed as a song by the author, Tolu' Akinyemi. Worthy of mention are my supporting crew, Aaron Lee and Jake Robson.)

Dad

Single moms know how hard it is.
Being a mother is a hard job.
Playing the dad is not all easy.
Be grateful, if you have a dad to call your own.

The Wedding Party

I dreamt of a glamorous wedding party,
A feature on the cover of Bellanaija.
Call me **Cindy** (short form of **Cinderella**).

I break *my bank* into pieces,
Intricate pieces.
My hashtag is #kolesheri2099.

A trending wedding
Seems to be trendy.
A miserable marriage is the *in-thing*.

We plan for the wedding,
Hire wedding planners.
We ignore the marriage.

Maybe it's not all that important,
I whisper to myself.
What if we hired *"marriage planners"*

To help us get it right before it becomes *broken pieces?*
Who will tell the young couple that there is more to marriage
Than a glamorous wedding party?

The Shoe

"I love Adidas," said Monalisa.
"My favourite was Nike and Puma", enthused *Michelle*.
Emeka's best-loved are designer shoes made in Aba,
The **China of Nigeria - our industrial powerhouse.**

We are lost in the glitz and glamour
Of the shoe. Adorning designers take precedence,
Swimming in the serenity of the applause—
Not the toe break, heavy legs, or the shoe pinch.

THE ROARS

The Roaring Lion

I told my younger self, "You're talented."
Self retorts, "I have no talent."
I squirm.
You're a baggage of talent.

Just unravel this gem;
Unravel this hidden gem.
We war against demons of **mediocrity;**
Demons who found a home in our head and hearts.

I told myself, "Dead Lions Don't Roar."
I shall not sleepwalk through life.
I shall wake!
I shall ROAR!

My younger self exclaims, "I believe,"
And I choose to nurture
And water every bit of my talent
So I don't **"sleepwalk"** through life.

Destiny

Our failures were gift wrapped
And we labeled them destiny.
We drank from the well of poor choices
And destiny became the "slaughter lamb."

Destiny was the whipping boy.
The boy who got a boot
And was contuse
As a result of that unfortunate *thing* called **destiny**.

Coming Back Soon

How I love my darling beau.
Among petals, I found my rose
As I walked through the lonely hills of bachelorhood.
I never knew life could be this good
And love as real.

As we walk through these lonely times,
I believe our love will stand true
As I fly skywards in pursuit of my dreams.
Let the words that I speak to you,
The affection so dear
And the love so true,
Be a guide to your every step
Coming back soon.

(This poem tells the story of a young man separated from his love.)

Blame Not The Devil

The Devil gets a bashing,
Many a times, from things we can control—
The Man who raped the two-year-old
Was the latest victim of the Devil?

Easy it seems, to pass the blame:
A little discipline
No ignominy to fathom
The belt loosening and boxer-removing devil has repented.

Blame not the Devil
When you have it all planned out.

Home

Home is not erect, like a statue.
It was where boys played on dusty roads.
Rolling tyres
And flying paper planes to new horizons.

Home was not erect, like a temple.
We carried homes in human bodies,
Conversing in diverse tongues
And building new families in hinterlands.

Home is not all about history.
It's the road where the past
Melts into the future.
Home is where dreams morph towards accomplishments.

Broken

We all are broken;
Broken in soul and spirit.
We all are broken;
Broken with words that pierce the heart.
We all are broken;
Tagged as no good through no fault of ours.
We all are broken;
Broken by a world filled with hate.
We all are broken—
"Broken but healing."

A Man Of Few Words

Hats off to the man of few words
Who sat behind those sacred corners
With an imaginary barrier, like Trump's border wall.

There was a man who hid behind smoke,
Vaped, and swallowed words
Like a toddler's toothpaste gobble.

There are days we drink from the well of silence,
Droplets of words like water with the familiar
Sound of tick-tock.

Like the sound of my antiquated wall clock.
Today, we send him off with words
Through these walls

With tongues that chorus "***speak out.***"
Build a castle with a war of words.
Let your rivers flow with a cistern of joy

Like a lil' baby
Sounding out
Dada, Mama.

No One Ever Told Me

No one ever told me I am proud.
This seems like music to my ears,
Music soon to be forgotten.
No one ever told me I am arrogant.

Tales by moonlight are like the days of old:
A tale soon to be erased.
No one ever told me the truth,
The truth so bitter, I loathe to hear
A deafening silence. The truth is scared.

Red Clover

We met on Red Clover,
Not on the road in Dover.
She sat in the back while I drove her
In my Range Rover.

We had a stopover.
It was late and I told her to sleep over.
My plan was to roll over
If only she could stay over.

Have a meal not like the Passover—
No drinks so we don't have hangovers.
Beg for our sins at the crossover.
Pretty hard to win her over.

Any mistake, it's all over.

(Inspired by project Red Clover, humorously adapted.)

Restitution

A dream that went in rubble,
Gone with the wind.
The grape that leaves the sour taste,
Never to be forgotten.
Dreams don't die.
Give me life and I will deliver the future back to you.
All that was taken will be restored to you.
This is my solemn promise.
I was naïve and young.
Now I am older and wiser.
I cannot turn back the hands of time
But I will correct the mistakes of my past.

(Dedicated to all those who have knowingly and unknowingly offended people and feel a need to make amends.)

Bleeding Heart

My heart bleeds,
Bleeds for hurt done to me.
My heart sinks;
Sinks as there is no one to fight my cause.

A friend she seems, to me
A foe, she proved to be.
The lioness had me for toast;
A toast with no savior in sight.

Who will give justice to the weak?
Justice seems not in sight.

Huggies

Not the diapers we all know.
An oxymoron, this should be known.
Cuddles and Hugs at will
Not like it will pay the bills.

Age not a barrier,
As long as she is not a carrier,
A cheerful giver
Not a penny or a fiver.

Lover of all
So long you can play ball.

(Inspired by Ayo Zubair. Your incessant hugging has not gone unnoticed.)

Before The Vows

Before you said I do
I was your one and only—
Breakfast in bed.

Romantic poems at night.
I was your very breath
Or so you made me believe.

You were heaven's gift to me.
How the times have changed!
I lay in bed longing for those nights before the vows.

Wake me up from this eerie dream
And bring me back to those glittering nights
Of unbridled love, before I said 'I do.'

The Parody Of Life

Exuding innocence, we came to the World.
With purity and virtue we joined the fold
Without a care in the World we lived our lives
Before the footprints were etched in our hearts.
Through the years we loved the World,
The allures and its pleasure a choice we made,
Not by our choice we came to stay.
Now, we find it hard to leave the World.
This is a satire the World should know.

Chemistry

If this was science, Life would be easier,
The chemical reaction permeating the laboratory of my
Heart, unbearable.
When the chemistry with the other guy evaporates
I will always be yours to have and cherish.

The light that shone through your eyes
Like firecrackers at Trafalgar Square on New Year's Eve
After my eyes took permanent residency
Behind your iris was *chemistry*.

My heart went on a rendezvous
With your fragile heart.
I built a temple and worshipped you all year long
This was *che-mis-try*.

I Will Be Yours

In the rough seas,
I will be there
Though the ocean's roar,
I will be there
When the sea waves sashay at us,
I will be there
Through the darkest of nights,
I will be your light
When you are weak and frail,
I will be your strength
Through thick and thin,
I will be yours.

(Dedicated to my loving wife; the wife of my youth.)

Tomorrow

The tenant today became a landlord 'tomorrow'.
Summer it was today, winter came 'tomorrow'.
A child today, an adult tomorrow
Like unto a new babe.

A day like no other
Possibilities unending
Poverty so aloud,
Obvious to the eyes.

Even the blind can see
All history
Thanks to tomorrow.

No

NO was the sacred word
Like a sacred cow.
Look here, "We take no prisoners."

NO took residence in mailbox accounts
Of job seekers
With rejection and dejection becoming
Companions like strange bedfellows.

NO is the synonym for bravery.
Broken boys call it Yes. You hear
Phrases like the "NO is just **shakara,"**
She will come around to say **"Yes".**
Moonwalk into your garden of truth
Live in your freeway of happiness.
Build up an arsenal of words
Land it like fatal blows.
Don't be afraid to drop the magic word **"NO".**

(Shakara means when someone is posing or showing off.)

Whatever Will Be, Will Not Be

Whatever will be, will not be.
If you laze away
Reaching for the stars
Without an effort

Things don't just happen.
Dreaming is not enough,
Sleep not away the future,
Whatever will be, will not be.

Wishful thinking is not an option,
The future is ours to make happen.

Emotional Abuse

The sacrileges many people are prone to commit
Hidden wounds,
Bleeding hearts the only markers.

Behind the laughter
Lies the cryptic sorrow
The mirrors can't tell.

The heart is broken;
The words spoken in haste
Are like daggers piercing through the soul.

Tell it among the heathens:
Words also soothe,
Edify, and build.

Wordsmith

I grew up learning about different vocations,
Goldsmith and Blacksmith.
There was a musician in my motherland
With the moniker 'Humblesmith.'

Being a wordsmith was ingenuity
Word weaving was a healing stream
We ate words over lunch
That tasted so sweet, like fruit punch.

We frame words like canvas hung on the wall,
Our heads and hearts make love,
A threesome with the brain.
We call it a pun.

We author books from small cubicles
We time travel into foreign lands
We are the battering ram at the village square
We are wordsmiths.

Talktalk

No need to go afar.
Unlimited talk time is
Like a network offering of choice,
Connection not a problem.

Everywhere you go
Hummingbirds can't compete,
Chattering on the latest gist in town.
Silence is golden,

Golden to those who treasure it.
A measure of silence is food for the soul.

Love At First Sight

A sight to behold
Beauty beyond comprehension
Melting even a heart of stone,
Grace and carriage in sync.

Sugar rushing through the belly
Goosebumps permeate through my heart:
A story never to be forgotten.
Love truly exists.

With you, it was at first sight.

Accent

The sister who travelled for a few weeks is back.
She travelled across the borders
With a voice as soothing as the angels,
A miracle as none I have seen.
Even the Queen seems to be in awe.
The hoarse voice has gotten some redemption.
Miracles do happen across the borders.

Grace

The undeserving leader in your sight,
The mere commissioner whom the Lord has blessed,
The contractor that gate-crashed the fixed termers' party,
All got there by grace.

Let's trash this thing called luck
In the recycle bin and call it **blessed.**
Let's exalt this oil
Not forgetting it's worth its weight in Gold.

Grace makes the race
Ace.

Grace - 2

Same lanterns
Different oils
Only the discerning will understand.

Efforts have limits
Strength encounters barriers
Connections fail for even the biggest of Men.

A language that permeates through the hearts of Kings
Makes Royalty of the Poor,
The door once closed, now ajar.

The rejected stone
Named the Chief Cornerstone
Grace makes all the difference.

Change

Change was the solemn anthem
That threw old men into a fit of rage
And crushed young men out of their reveries.

Change sent us into strange lands
With shattered songs
And broken chords.

Change was a pit of lies
Clothed in the garment of deceit
And fuelled by power mongers.

Change in itself is not a ruse.
Change found a home in quirky tongues
And language habitually tainted,

Tainted by the corruption of men,
Promises of change all a dream.
Clueless about the change touted from the rooftops,

Change is now scorned in the street corners,
An abomination no one wants to hear.

Ideas Rule The World

Ideas were legacies
Like the Sahara Desert metamorphosing
Into a galaxy
A holiday haven.

Ideas were crisp like banknotes.
No money, no problem.
Great ideas are currencies,
The value no one can despise.

Ideas have made the World a better place,
Great inventions the seed thereof.
One great idea at a time
Will change the World in leaps and bounds.

Peak

Peak of Quality
Quality Renowned
From far and near
An acclaim to treasure.

Peak of Value
Value the years can't erode.
Like the old
Wisdom comes with the years,
Heights and Depths the competition trembles.

Peak of Originality
Not a tale
Or a gimmick,
Imitation not a choice.

Peak of capacity
Bright minds
Great ideas
Minerals and vitamins in abundance.

Reach for your peak
As a home without peak
Lacks memories pleasant to cherish.

(Dedicated to the long-standing brand in the Nigerian Dairy Sector, Peak Milk.)

Cap Without A Head

We were boys with dreams
Dreams birthed from spring of ideas.
Our dreams evaporated as soon as they were
Conjured.

They called us **headless** chickens
In the rapper's voice, *"men without glory."*
We wake. We toil. We fight.

In my environs *"I see silver spoon kids,"*
The *ajebutter* who had luxuries at their
beck and call.
Mess it all up.

I pick one. Two.
Used my last card from the packed crowd.
I tower. I rise.
I live to fight another day.

(**Ajebutter** is a popular term used by Nigerians in describing a spoilt
kid or weakling.)

Inspired by an African Proverb: "Some people have Heads without a
Cap while some others have Caps without a head."

Education

Education was the gateway
That birthed getaways
Into foreign lands
And beautiful cities.

Education took me far away from the ladder
Of ignorance
Into big edifices and cured me from the
Malady of poverty and living on the periphery.

My Woman

She was heaven on earth
And our love affair was a rhapsody
Of realities.

My love for her was ecstasy.
We built a future on Fantasy Island
Together. Forever. That's legacy.

Arm's Length

Let's obfuscate them from radar,
Take them away from arm's length,
Those sons of Golgotha.

Let their fiery words birth in us new life.
Let their words be the impetus
That will lead us into our calvary,

Those word-swinging miscreants.
They killed me
Yes, they did.

I have learnt to dance in the hailstorm,
Buzzing around like a firefly,
Free from the prison of those word-swinging miscreants.
I Roar!

Bio

Tolu' Akinyemi is an exceptional talent and an out-of-the box creative thinker; a change management agent and a leader par excellence. Tolu' is a business analyst and financial crime consultant as well as a Certified Anti-Money Laundering Specialist (CAMS) with extensive experience working with leading Investment Banks and Consultancy Firms. Tolu' is also a personal development and career coach and a prolific writer with more than 10 years' writing experience. He is a mentor to hundreds of young people. He worked as an Associate Mentor in St Mary's School, Cheshunt and as an Inclusion Mentor at Barnwell School, Stevenage in the United Kingdom, helping students raise their aspirations and standards of performance and helping them cope with transitions from one educational stage to another.

A man whom many refer to as "Mr Vision," he is a trained economist from Ekiti State University, formerly known as University of Ado-Ekiti (UNAD). He sat his Masters' Degree in Accounting and Financial Management at the University of Hertfordshire, Hatfield, United Kingdom. Tolu' was a student ambassador at the University of Hertfordshire, Hatfield, representing the University in major forums and engaging with young people during various assignments.

Tolu' Akinyemi is a home-grown talent; an alumnus of the Daystar Leadership Academy (DLA). He is passionate about people and wealth creation. He believes strongly that life is about impacting others. In his words, "To have a secure future, we must be willing to pay the price in order to earn the prize." Tolu' has headlined and featured in various Open Slam, Poetry Slam, Spoken Word, and Open Mic events in and outside the United Kingdom. He also inspires large audiences through spoken word performances, he has appeared as a keynote speaker in major forums and events, and he facilitates creative writing master classes to all types of audiences.

Tolu' Akinyemi was born in Ado-Ekiti, Nigeria and currently lives in the United Kingdom. Tolu' is an ardent supporter of the Chelsea Football Club, London.

You can connect with Tolu' on his various Social Media Accounts:
Instagram: @ToluToludo
Facebook: facebook.com/toluaakinyemi
Twitter: @ToluAkinyemi

Author's Note

Thank you for the time you have taken to read this book. I do hope you enjoyed the poems in it.

If you loved the book and have a minute to spare, I would really appreciate a short review on the page or site where you bought the book. Your help in spreading the word is greatly appreciated. Reviews from readers like you make a huge difference to helping new readers decide to get the book.

Thank you!

Tolu' Akinyemi

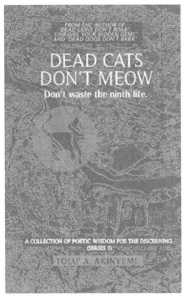

116

Printed in Poland
by Amazon Fulfillment
Poland Sp. z o.o., Wrocław

58028640R00078